To Dylan

Enjoy!

The Reluctant Butterfly

DEBRA COLLETT

Illustrated by Carrie Pearce

Deb'Collett

Carrie Pearce

WestBow Press books may be ordered through booksellers or by contacting:

WestBow Press
A Division of Thomas Nelson
1663 Liberty Drive
Bloomington, IN 47403
www.westbowpress.com
1-(866) 928-1240

Because of the dynamic nature of the Internet, any web addresses or links contained in this book may have changed since publication and may no longer be valid. The views expressed in this work are solely those of the author and do not necessarily reflect the views of the publisher, and the publisher hereby disclaims any responsibility for them.

Any people depicted in stock imagery provided by Thinkstock are models, and such images are being used for illustrative purposes only.

Certain stock imagery © Thinkstock.

ISBN: 978-1-4908-1245-8 (sc)
ISBN: 978-1-4908-1246-5 (e)

Library of Congress Control Number: 2013918602

Printed in the United States of America.

WestBow Press rev. date: 11/04/2013

WestBow
PRESS
A DIVISION OF THOMAS NELSON

"There is no fear in love, but perfect love casts out fear . . ."

1 John 4:18
ESV

Once upon a time there was a caterpillar named Little Lou.
She was born on a sunny warm day in the springtime.

Little Lou loved her world!
She lived in a big garden with her best friend, Ladybug.
Spring grew into summer. Little Lou felt so warm and safe! She loved
creeping from plant to plant across the moist, rich soil. Little Lou munched
away on the green leaves while Ladybug ate aphids.

One day, Little Lou noticed Butterfly fluttering overhead. "Hello, Butterfly!" called out Little Lou. "How are you today?"
"I am well," said Butterfly.

Then Butterfly asked the caterpillar a very important question. "Are you ready for THE BIG CHANGE, Little Lou?"
"What is THE BIG CHANGE?" asked Little Lou.

Butterfly answered her, "Soon you will turn into a butterfly and sip nectar from flowers.

You will be like Me."

Little Lou was *afraid*.

As quick as she could, Little Lou inched and wriggled over to Ladybug.
"Ladybug! Ladybug!" she cried. "Butterfly says I am going to change!
I don't want to sip nectar from flowers!
I want to eat leaves."
"Oh, Little Lou," replied Ladybug,
"I'm so sorry you feel so upset -
I thought you knew
you would become a butterfly.
Are you sure you didn't know this?

Little Lou frowned.
She thought,
and then thought some more.
"I guess I did know it –
but I didn't pay attention,
because I didn't want it to be true,"
she finally admitted.
"Why don't you talk to The Butterfly again?"
suggested Ladybug.
"He's been there before you. He can help you."
Little Lou felt very mixed-up inside.
Her tummy hurt like she had eaten too many leaves, but she knew it wasn't
from any plant.
She crawled off to be alone.

Then, even before she could call out for him,
Butterfly landed quietly beside her.
"Hello," said Butterfly.
"Hello," replied Little Lou.
They sat together for a while in silence.

"Being a caterpillar is all I know. I don't want to stop eating leaves!
I'm scared of heights - I don't want to fly!" confessed Little Lou.
"You were designed for more than crawling and
leaves, Little Lou," responded The Butterfly.
"THE BIG CHANGE will come - even if you don't want it to occur."
"But I don't want everything to change," complained the tiny caterpillar.

"Well, 'everything' doesn't change - but you do."
Butterfly continued, "The world will go on very much as it is. The garden will still be big and green in the summer. Ladybug will still eat aphids. The sun will rise and set in its course. But you will change completely, and forever. Once THE BIG CHANGE occurs, it cannot be undone."

"Does it hurt?" asked Little Lou.

"Sometimes," answered Butterfly honestly. "But how scary it feels when you go through it depends a lot on you."

After talking to Butterfly for a long time, Little Lou felt better. Later, she told her friend Ladybug all about it.

Ladybug promised,
"I can't go through it for you, but I will be there with you." Little
Lou was grateful for her friend. "Thank you," she said.

Summer turned to fall, and Little Lou began to stuff herself with leaves.
"Last chance," she said to herself, "might as well make the most of it."
Before she knew it, Butterfly came and declared
it was time for THE BIG CHANGE.
"I also wanted to say goodbye to you, Little Lou."
"GOODBYE?!?" cried the startled caterpillar.

"Yes." Butterfly continued, "You cannot follow me the way you are right now, but after THE BIG CHANGE we will be more alike than ever. Then I will come back for you, and you will follow me. I promise."

Little Lou panicked. "So I have to do this all alone?" Little Lou asked, her voice shaky with fear.

"Not exactly," explained Butterfly. "There are some things that must be done that only you can do, but you have everything I taught you inside you now, and Ladybug will be nearby. No one is ever completely alone."

Little Lou was not sure that made her feel better, but she decided to trust The Butterfly.

It was time. Little Lou wove her cocoon.

Ladybug kept her promise and watched over Little Lou as best she could.
The day came when Ladybug couldn't watch anymore; it was nearly winter
and she had to hibernate to protect herself.
"Goodbye, Little Lou!" cried Ladybug.

But Little Lou couldn't answer. Inside her cocoon, Little Lou began to
change. She was scared, sometimes so scared that she thought that she
could shake like jelly. Then she realized that she actually *had* turned into a
little glop of jelly!

But Butterfly had told her this would be
so, and she hung onto his promise that
THE BIG CHANGE
would be for the better.
Little Lou remembered
a very important part of what
Butterfly had explained:
Some steps of THE BIG CHANGE
were things she had to do, and
some steps were things she
simply allowed to happen –
she did not have to do any work
at all.

Little Lou felt herself swallowed up by
The Great Silence.
Nothing was the same.
As a matter of fact, she *became* nothing - not even scared.
The winter was very deep, cold, and long.
But somewhere in the chill, Lou began to dream of sipping flowers.
Winter passed and spring came again - as it always does.

Through the mesh of her cocoon, Lou heard
a muffled noise.
"Lou! Lou! Are you still there?"
It was Ladybug!

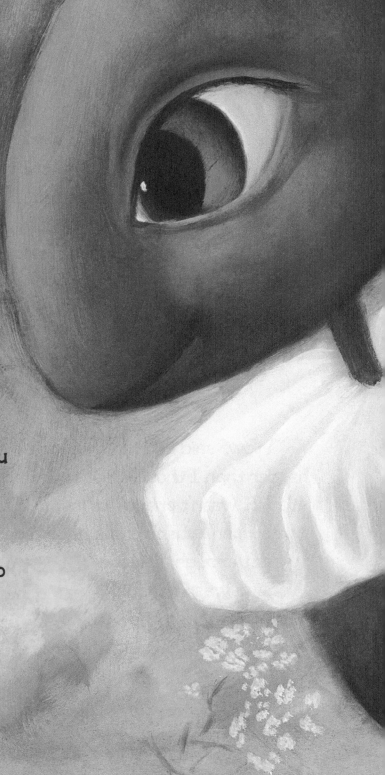

"I'm here!" shouted Lou.
"I'm coming!"
She began to struggle.
"Help me out, Ladybug!" cried Lou.
"No," answered another voice.
It was a beautiful voice, more rich and
sweet than anything
she had ever heard,
but somehow very familiar.
Lou stopped a moment, trying to
remember . . .
"Butterfly!" yelled Lou.
"Yes, I'm here, Lou, just as I promised.
You are a butterfly now, too, but only you
can act like it.
Your first task is to break out of your
cocoon. You must do it yourself –
wiggling out is what allows your wings to
work!
You don't want to have gone through
THE BIG CHANGE
for nothing, do you?"

It was hard work, but Little Lou finally pulled
herself all the way out of the cocoon.
Ladybug giggled. "You're all wet and wrinkly!"
"Whew! I'm pooped!" sighed Lou.
"Get some rest," said Butterfly. "I will guard you."
Lou and Ladybug took a nap.

"Wow," said Lou to Ladybug after they woke up, "That was longer and
harder than I thought! Just when I figured I was done, there was one more
step. It wasn't enough to just eat leaves; I had to spin my cocoon. Staying in
the cocoon, wasn't enough, I needed to be transformed. Being transformed
wasn't enough, I needed to work my way out of that comfortable cocoon.
Working wasn't enough, I also needed to rest. *All* of it made me a butterfly."
Lou stretched and yawned, admiring her wings. She looked around. The
garden was again big and green, and Ladybug was munching on an aphid.

Lou turned to Butterfly, "I understand what you mean now. Everything is the same, but it all looks and feels different because I am different."

Butterfly smiled at her, and Lou smiled back.
And then, Lou laughed. "Come on, Ladybug! I'm
hungry and want to sip some flowers.

Let's fly somewhere new!"

Debra Collett is an instinctive encourager who has lived the truth of 1 John 4:18: " . . . [that] perfect love casts out fear." She graduated cum laude from Moody Bible Institute with a BS in Biblical Studies and also has certifications in emergency management. A Central Illinois native, Debra can often be found hiking and enjoying the company of ladybugs, caterpillars, and butterflies. This is her third book.

Visit her online at debracollett.com.

Illustrator **Carrie Pearce** was inspired by DaVinci's portrait of Ginevra de' Benci to develop a look she describes as "expressive realism." She resides in her hometown of Peoria, Illinois. Now a nationally acclaimed artist, Carrie began with a Walt Disney light-up table and asking her mom to draw her pictures as Carrie described them to her. Carrie is very excited to have now fulfilled her dream of illustrating a children's book.

Visit her online at carriepearce.com.

CPSIA information can be obtained at www.ICGtesting.com
Printed in the USA
LVOW02s1136141113

360969LV00002B/8/P